The
Isle of Wight Revisited

A Collection of photographs produced from
the original glass plate negatives

by
Colin Fairweather & Alan Stroud

THE OAKWOOD PRESS

© Oakwood Press & Colin Fairweather & Alan Stroud 2005

British Library Cataloguing in Publication Data
A Record for this book is available from the British Library
ISBN 0 85361 642 6

Typeset by Oakwood Graphics.
Repro by Pkmediaworks, Cranborne, Dorset.
Printed by The Amadeus Press, Cleckheaton, Yorkshire.

For Rose and Sue

Published by The Oakwood Press (Usk), P.O. Box 13, Usk, Mon., NP15 1YS.
E-mail: sales@oakwoodpress.co.uk
Website: www.oakwoodpress.co.uk

Contents

Introduction

We would like to think that this book of photographs, dating from the mid-1890s to the 1920s, is unique. Every photograph in this book has been produced from the original glass plate negative, or in some cases, a positive 'magic lantern' slide. Unlike other local interest publications, not a single paper print or postcard has been used in the compilation of this album; every photograph in this book, without exception, has been produced by scanning the original glass plates with the aid of computer technology. The pictures have been chosen, not simply to accompany text, but to stand on their own photographic merits. Most now have historical interest but they have also been taken by people who had an eye for a good picture, even though the subject, at the time, may have appeared mundane. Some of them were quite clearly taken simply for their artistic merit. The photographs of the garden archway, the river scene, and Newchurch valley, for instance, were not taken as a historical record but because the photographer recognised their pictorial qualities.

The fact that this book exists at all is due largely to a series of fortunate events over the last 30 years. As amateur photographers in the late 1960s and 1970s we had always realised the importance of recording everyday life with our own cameras, for the enjoyment of future generations. Consequently, whenever we were given the chance to acquire the seemingly unimportant work of early photographers, we did so wherever possible.

Over the following 30 years, negatives came to us from all manner of sources. Some had literally been left out for the dustman while others were bought by us as a result of placing a series of 'wanted ads' in local newspapers. On one occasion, following a tip off, we arrived only to find that some of the images had already been removed from the glass with a scouring pad to be used for picture framing or as cloches. On another occasion we were only just in time as the negatives offered to us were literally on the point of destruction, having been kept in extremely damp conditions and had reached the point where the image emulsion was actually slipping off the glass. Some, however, were successfully rescued from such a fate and with a degree of conservation have now been restored.

The negatives are the work of seven, possibly more, generally unknown photographers; the exception to this being those of William R. Hogg, a name well known to today's vintage postcard collectors. Hogg was a photographic postcard producer from Ryde, who also owned and ran George Street Post Office. There is naturally therefore, a greater percentage of Hogg's work in this book than that of any other contributor. Readers can assume that most of the photographs of the East Wight area are the work of Hogg.

By the early 20th century, amateur photographers were beginning to turn to the newly introduced, roll-film cameras which had made photography more affordable. Professional photographers and the more wealthy amateurs,

A 'National' half-plate format camera.

however, continued to produce images using 'stand' and 'field' cameras, precision engineered from wood and brass. Typically, a half-plate camera of this nature could be bought for £5 0s. 0d., or £11 10s. 0d. with a higher quality lens. To put this price in perspective, in 1900 a builder's labourer earnt 4d. per hour and a policeman on the Island was earning £70 per annum so quite clearly a camera of this nature would be beyond their means.

For those that could afford them, these glass plate cameras were highly technical instruments that not only allowed accurate focusing but were also capable of 'movements' of the lens and, or, the film plane. There are many types of lens movement including tilt, swing and 'rising front', that correct optical distortions of the image. For example, some readers may be aware of the annoying phenomenon of converging verticals that can plague modern photography. This can be corrected by raising the lens vertically, but parallel, to the film plane. Because of the sheer size and weight of these cameras, they were almost always mounted on a sturdy wooden tripod adding many pounds of weight to the already heavy kit that had to be transported to every location. Spontaneous, hand-held shots were almost out of the question, each shot having to be meticulously composed and subject to a rigid set of routine procedures before an exposure could be attempted.

Instead of the luxury of a modern 36 exposure film cassette, or the seemingly inexhaustible capacity of a digital memory card, these early photographers were only armed with half a dozen or so 'dark slides' which were simple, flat, light-tight containers pre-loaded with one, or in the case of double-sided slides, two unexposed glass negatives. Underneath the focusing cloth, the photographer was presented with an image, both vertically and horizontally reversed, projected onto a frosted glass screen at the rear of the camera. Focusing and lens adjustments were carried out, the dark slide, loaded with an unexposed plate, was now inserted in front of the screen and after closing, or capping, the shutter, the safety slide could now be withdrawn, thereby presenting the light-sensitive emulsion towards the lens, ready to capture the image. Exposure times were lengthy by modern standards due to the slow sensitivity of the emulsion, equivalent perhaps, to ISO (ASA) 8 or 10 with a corresponding 'instantaneous' speed in the order of 1/10th or 1/20th of a second. This long exposure would often result in blurred images due to subject movement or camera shake. This was minimised in later years with the advent of more sensitive plates and by the aid of add-on shutter timing units. Although these negatives were obviously for the production of monochrome images, the emulsions used were colour-sensitive, usually to the detriment of the image. For example, unlike today's 'panchromatic' black and white films, sensitive to all colours, these emulsions were 'orthochromatic' and highly sensitive to the blue end of the visible spectrum but were partially blind to the red end. This could result in unnaturally dark skin tones and, in particular, disappointingly white skies as stunning clouds and vivid blue skies merged together to form one mass of the same featureless tone.

Glass plate negatives generally ranged in size from 3½ in. x 2½ in. up to a massive 20 in. x 24 in. or even bigger. Most of the glass negatives in our collection are what is known as 'half-plate' format and measure 6½ in. x 4¾ in. whilst the remainder are mostly 'quarter-plate', measuring 4¼ in. x 3¼ in. It is worth noting here that each of the half-plates has a surface area equivalent to 20 modern day 35mm negatives. Correspondingly, each half-plate negative could, in theory, be enlarged to 4 ft x 3 ft and yet still be of a better resolution than a 12 in. x 8 in. print from one of today's better 35mm or digital cameras.

At the turn of the last century, when most of these images were produced, it would have been common practice to produce 'contact prints' which were made by placing the previously developed negative on top of a sheet of light sensitive photographic paper in a darkened room and then exposing the layered 'sandwich', briefly, to high intensity light, usually a tungsten bulb. On developing the paper, an identically sized, positive print would be produced, consequently, most photographers of this period hardly ever saw their work enlarged and sadly, were unable to appreciate the full beauty and quality of their images. Ironically, the most technically capable of the photographers whose work is displayed here, W.R. Hogg, although using the larger half plate format which produced the highest quality negatives was actually losing 33 per cent of each image by cropping the picture to fit the standard postcard-size format of 3½ in. x 5½ in. Consequently, this means that for the first time, these Hogg images are now being seen in their entirety and in optimum quality.

As far back as 1980, we were aware that we had the beginnings of a book but were daunted by the prospect of producing high quality prints by the conventional wet darkroom method. These giant negatives require the use of a correspondingly giant enlarger and the ability to use it. We had neither at that point. We found a 100-year-old enlarger in a local junk shop and converted it from rather hazardous, high current, carbon arc lighting to safer modern tungsten bulb illumination. We were then able to produce prints with limited success but found that retouching blemishes and scratches was a major problem requiring excessive time and effort and the results were disappointing at times.

The arrival of personal computers, scanners and powerful photo-editing programmes has solved these problems. The computer has allowed us to retouch and repair the negatives with ease, to a degree that our contributors could not have dreamed of but would surely have appreciated. The dilemma, of course, is when does legitimate photo repair become a work of fiction? It would be all too easy to insert a 21st century sky into the photographs to overcome the previously mentioned tonal problems or to falsify images by the addition or removal of other details. For us, the answer was never in doubt. We wanted to retain the historical integrity of the images and consequently we have restricted our editing activities to contrast correction where necessary and the repair of scratches and blemishes. The images in the book are what the photographers saw in their viewfinders and for us too, the image has always been paramount.

Glass plates in their original boxes complete with handwritten labels.

With this in mind we knew that we had to present them in as large a format as possible and that this dictated no more than one image per page, with the narrowest of borders. This has also meant that with a landscape format book the portrait format images inevitably have had to be presented in such a way that they have to be viewed by turning the book through 90 degrees. The alternative would have been to either crop those images drastically and unnaturally, or to print two smaller images on one page. We hope this small inconvenience will be seen as worthwhile in order to appreciate the images to the full. Most of the other photographs fell naturally into a landscape format but some, due to their composition and quality, demanded a double page panoramic treatment. In every case, we have restricted ourselves to adding only a title and plate number, the full captions being located in the index section at the back of the book. After considering all of the alternatives, we feel this choice of layout style offers the best compromise.

The captions vary in length because some pictures speak for themselves, requiring only location details etc. In other cases we have supported the photographs with facts, quotes and extracts which we hope will prove both informative and interesting. We have tried our very best to be accurate but if you are able to correct any captions or supply further information about any of the photographs in this book, particularly the unknown locations, please contact us via Oakwood Press.

The digital age has enabled us to revisit the analogue world of Victorian and Edwardian photographers of the Isle of Wight. Almost certainly, all of the contributors to this book would have embraced computer technology as an aid to photo-editing, just as we have. None of them, however, would have contemplated parting with their high resolution plate cameras. They, like us, would prefer the archival permanence of their silver halide negatives to the possibly ephemeral nature of digital storage methods with their ever changing file extensions. Glass negatives, barring accidents, will be here forever; electronic images can disappear at the click of a button.

In 1986, to celebrate the 900th anniversary of the Domesday book, a new one was created using the work of thousands of contributors across Britain and was stored on 12 inch laser disc. Today there are no working players left and the entire work is unreadable. The discs seem set to remain inaccessible for ever as the format, like the Domesday book itself, is now part of history.

We would do well, also, to remember the planned redundancy of VHS, the obsolescence of 8 track audio cassettes and Betamax video, and the increasingly mounting evidence of the instability of the CD format. Negatives, glass plate or film, have already stood the test of time. Tried and tested, they will be just as accessible in the next 100 years for future generations to revisit; as they no doubt will.

Fig 1. Under the photographer's cloth, the image, seen here on a 'National' camera, was displayed on a ground glass screen where it was viewed upside down.

Fig 2. Prior to taking the photograph, the ground glass viewfinder is swung away to allow the 'double dark slide', containing two unexposed glass negatives, one on each side, to be slid into place.

THE NATISONAL.

¶These outfits comprise a well-finished mahogany camera, double dark slide, lens, shutter and tripod.

The camera has every up - to - date movement, including universal swing front rack and pinion wide - angle movement, etc.

The front is built extra large and the bellows almost square, so that when the extreme rise of the front is used, there is little possibility of a cut - off.

MODEL 4a Double-Extension.	$\frac{1}{4}$-plate	$\frac{1}{2}$-plate	1/1-plate
With Aldis Uno Anastigmat, f/7.7	£2 17 6	£3 10 0	£6 0 0
Primus Rapid Rectilinear, f/8..........	2 5 0	3 0 0	4 12 6
Beck Rapid Symmetrical, f/8...........	2 10 0	3 5 0	5 0 0
" Mutar Anastigmat, Series II, f/6	4 2 6	5 7 6	----
Dallmeyer Stigmatic IV, f/6.3..........	5 0 0	6 15 0	----
Cooke Anastigmat III, f/6.6.............	6 2 6	8 5 0	14 10 0
Goerz Dagor III, f/6.8....................	7 5 0	10 10 0	14 10 0

MODEL 4, Triple-Extension.	$\frac{1}{2}$-plate	1/1-plate
Aldis "Uno" Anastigmat, f/7.7	£4 0 0	£6 17 6
" Primus " R.R. Lens	3 10 0	5 10 0
Beck Symmetrical. f/8.....................	3 15 0	5 17 6
Beck Mutar, Series II f/6....................	5 17 6	8 10 0
Goerz Anastigmat, III, f/6.8............................	10 10 0	15 7 6

MODEL 5. Brass-Bound.	$\frac{1}{2}$-plate	1/1-plate
Aldis " Uno " Anastigmat, f/7.7....................	£5 0 0	£8 2 6
" Primus " Rapid Rectilinear Lens.................	4 10 0	6 15 0
Beck Symmetrical, f/8....................	4 15 0	7 2 6
Beck Mutar, Series II, f/6....................	6 17 6	----
Goerz Anastigmat, Series III, f/6.8...................	11 10 0	16 12 6

Fig 3. An advertisement for the 'National' camera in the 1913 almanac of The British Journal of Photography.

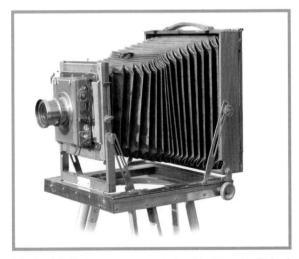

Fig 4. A half-plate camera manufactured by Thornton Pickard. The lens is mounted on to the camera via a roller blind shutter unit. This brought to an end the practice of exposing the photograph by manually removing and replacing the lens hood.

Fig 5. The lens and shutter panel is seen in its raised position. This 'rising front' facility was utilised to correct converging verticals and allowed the tops of tall buildings to be included in the frame without tilting the camera off vertical.

Fig 6. By way of comparison, a half-plate glass negative measuring 6½ in. x 4¾ in. is shown alongside a strip of four 35 mm negatives.

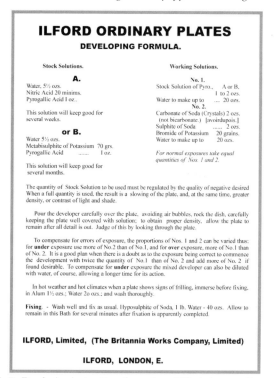

Fig 7. Developing instructions from a box of Ilford glass negatives.

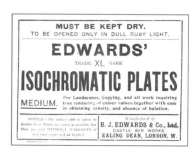

Fig 8. A selection of labels from the lids of boxes of glass plates.

Fig 9. Part of Plate 51 showing damage and minor scratches on the original glass negative.

Fig 10. The same area after restoration using a computer photo-editing programme.

Plate 1: Horse-drawn Coaches, Esplanade, Ryde.

Plate 2: Upper Union Street, Ryde.

Plate 3: The Royal Pier Hotel, Ryde.

Plate 4: Entrance to the Pier, Ryde.

Plate 5: Newchurch Valley.

Plate 6: View from Mount Joy, Newport.

Plate 7: View from Carisbrooke Castle.

Plate 8: River Scene, Unknown Location.

Plate 9: The Trincomalee at Anchor, Cowes.

Plate 10: The Pier, Alum Bay.

Plate 11: The Cliffs, Alum Bay.

Plate 12: Seagrove Bay.

Plate 13: Pier Road, Seaview.

Plate 14: The Slipway, Seaview.

Plate 15: Seagrove Bay, Seaview.

Plate 16: Seaview Pier.

Plate 17: The Toll Road, Seaview.

Plate 18: PS Duchess of Kent leaving Ryde Pier.

Plate 19: Crowds on Rude Pier.

Plate 20: Day Trippers, Ryde Pier.

Plate 21: PS Lorna Doone.

Plate 22: PS Prince of Wales.

Plate 23: Garden Archway, Unknown Location.

Plate 24: Fernhill House, Wootton.

Plate 25: House Interior, Unknown Location.

Plate 26: House Interior, Unknown Location.

Plate 27: Theatre Royal, Ryde.

Plate 28: The Royal Victoria Yacht Club, Ryde.

Plate 29: St Thomas Square and Union Street, Ryde.

Plate 30: River Medina, St Cross, Newport.

Plate 31: Little London, Newport.

Plate 32: The Harbour, Newport.

Plate 33: River Medina, Dodnor.

Plate 34: Cargo Ship, River Medina.

Plate 35: The Black Horse Inn, George Street, Ryde.

Plate 36: Pier Street, Ryde.

Plate 37: The Hand in Hand, Nelson Place, Ryde.

Plate 38: The New Inn, Brighstone.

48

Plate 39: The Fleming Arms, Binstead.

Plate 40: Lower High Street, Ryde.

Plate 41: The Prince of Wales, High Street, Ryde.

Plate 42: The Vine, Ryde.

Plate 43: The Strand Hotel, Ryde.

Plate 44: The Hare and Hounds, Arreton.

Plate 45: The White Lion, Niton.

Plate 46: Advertisement Hoarding, St John's Road Bridge, Ryde.

Plate 47: Evans and Dyke, Ryde.

Plate 48: The Dore Sisters, Warwick Street, Ryde.

Plate 49: Temperance Hotel, Ryde.

Plate 50: Washhouse, Unknown Location.

Plate 51: Railway Agents, George Street, Ryde.

Plate 52: Pickfords Office, Esplanade, Ryde.

Plate 53: Heath's Store, The Broadway, Totland.

Plate 54: Lower Union Street, Ryde.

Plate 55: St John's Road Bridge, Ryde.

Plate 56: Upper High Street, Ryde.

Plate 57: The High Street, Carisbrooke.

Plate 58: Castle Street Ford, Carisbrooke.

Plate 59: The Church and Bell Inn, Godshill.

Plate 60: High Street and Square, Brading.

Plate 61: IWCR Railway Station, Shide.

Plate 62: Binstead Hill.

Plate 63: Denmark Road School, Cowes.

Plate 64: View from St Thomas Church, Newport.

Plate 65: View from St Thomas Church, Newport.

Plate 66: The Toll Bridge, Yarmouth.

Plate 67: The Square, Yarmouth.

Plate 68: The Royal Spithead Hotel, Bembridge.

Plate 69: The High Street, Sandown.

Plate 70: The High Street, Newport.

Plate 71: The Town Hall, Newport.

Plate 72: St Thomas Square, Newport.

Plate 73: Railway Viaduct, Newport.

Plate 74: FY&N Railway Station, Carisbrooke.

Plate 75: FY&N Railway Station, Calbourne.

Plate 76: IWCR Railway Station, Newport.

Plate 77: Railway Tunnel, St Lawrence.

Plate 78: IWR Railway Station, Ventnor.

Plate 79: Railway Crossing, Alvington.

Plate 80: Medina Railway Jetty, Cowes.

Plate 81: IWCR Railway Station, Cowes.

Plate 82: Union Street, Ryde.

Plate 83: Clifford's Gate, Spencer Road, Ryde.

Plate 84: Gilling's, Station Road, Freshwater.

Plate 85: The York Hotel, George Street, Ryde.

Plate 86: The Hunt in St James Square, Newport.

Plate 87: The Hunt on The Downs.

Plate 88: The Hunt at Calbourne.

Plate 89: The Racecourse, Ashey.

Plate 90: Stuck in the Mud.

Plate 91: IWCR Rolling Stock, Newport.

Plate 92: Bus Garage Fire, Somerton, Cowes.

Plate 93: Roman Villa, Newport.

Plate 94: The Keep, Carisbrooke Castle.

108

Plate 95: Abbey Ruins, Quarr.

Plate 96: IW Museum, Quay Street, Newport.

Plate 97: Beach Scene, Unknown Location.

Plate 98: The Cascade, Ventnor.

112

Plate 99: The Carnival, Ventnor.

Plate 100: Old Soldier and Dog.

Plate 101: St Boniface Church, Bonchurch.

Plate 102: The Regatta, Seaview.

1 Horse-drawn coaches, Esplanade, Ryde.
On the left, a horse and coach of the Royal Blue Line, weighed down with passengers, is ready to pull away. Like the Royal Pier Hotel across the road, its days were numbered due to the imminent arrival of the motor car. *'Carriage Fares. By Distance - 1/- any distance within the borough (except for a few outlying parts). By time – 3/- per hour for one-horse carriages, 4/- per hour for two-horse carriages.'* - Ward Lock Guide Book 1912.

2 Upper Union Street, Ryde.
Like a great deal of Ryde, Union Street is of Georgian origin and fortunately it has managed to retain its charm. Something that has changed, however, is the traffic flow which was two-way in the early 1900s, when this photograph was taken. The bus making its way up the hill is one of those brought over to the Island by the IOW Motor Express Syndicate to replace their double-deckers which had been defeated by the Island's steep inclines. *(See Plate 3.)*

3 The Royal Pier Hotel, Ryde.
This huge hotel became a nuisance, its location at the bottom of Union Street causing hold ups and accidents as vehicles turned the sharp corner into Pier Street. The council bought it in 1932 to demolish it. Waiting for customers are three of the four new double-deckers, which were used to start the first regular bus service on the Island in 1905. They proved not to be powerful enough for the Island's hills and after six months were replaced by single-deckers.

4 Entrance to the Pier, Ryde.
In 1875 the railway from Newport reached Ryde, but only as far as St Johns Road. From there, a horse-drawn tram took passengers to the Pier Head. The slow tram was quite unable to cope with large numbers of passengers and became a source of frustration to the LBSCR and LSWR, who jointly ran the Portsmouth to Ryde ferries and wanted to be able to sell through tickets to the Island. They eventually took matters into their own hands and in 1880 extended the railway line from St Johns to the Pier Head.

5 Newchurch Valley.
Someone with an eye for a pastoral scene took this photograph from the road over Mersley Down, somewhere on the stretch between the Hare and Hounds and Ashey Down. The white smudge, nearly centre, is a train leaving Newchurch station for Sandown. Above it is the spire of the church at Newchurch.

6 View from Mount Joy, Newport.
This photograph presents some odd perspectives. Behind St Thomas Church is the Town Hall clock tower and to the right of that, the warehouses on Newport Quay. The open fields behind them are what we now know as Seaclose Park. Down river on the western bank, past Newport Rowing Club and the Ship and Launch Inn, the Cement Mills at Stag Lane are visible.

7 View from Carisbrooke Castle.
The lane in the centre of the photograph is Priory Lane with its duck pond just visible. To the right of it, behind the trees, is Carisbrooke station. The lane today is barely recognisable, surrounded on both sides by housing instead of fields. Left foreground is Kent's Mill, complete with oast house which milled until 1939 and was once one of the largest trading mills of the Island. It was described in 1967 as, *'in a sorry state now'*, but has since been restored as a private residence.

8 River Scene, Unknown Location.
An excellent, well composed photograph of an atmospheric scene. It is just possible that this is the River Medina at the Shide end of the stretch of river that runs from there to Blackwater, as the glass negative for this photograph was accompanied by a series taken of Shide station and crossing.

9 The *Trincomalee* at Anchor, Cowes.
This was in an envelope marked 'Trincomalee at Lallows Yard, Cowes, about 1897. Paskins lobster boat in front' (Paskins was a Cowes fish shop which traded into the 1970s.) Why she was anchored here is a mystery. She was built in 1807 in Bombay, and after a long career in the Navy was saved from the scrap yard, to be renamed the *Foudroyant*. She was still owned by the Navy in 1987 and ended up at Portsmouth. The *Trincomalee* now lives on, preserved, in Hartlepool.

10 The Pier, Alum Bay.
The pier opened in 1887, costing £2,135, with a cafe, gift shop and a restaurant onshore. It flourished, as did most piers, and in its heyday steamers operated countless services to South Coast resorts. The beginning of the end came in 1927 when the pier was broken in two by storms and was put beyond economical repair. The remaining section stayed in operation until it became a military practice area in World War II and was reduced to girders.

11 The Cliffs, Alum Bay.
The pier was situated where the chair lift platform is today. To the right, the ladies are filling souvenir glass ornaments with coloured sand. *'Alum Bay derives its name from the alum found there. The cliffs are beautifully variegated ... with sands of different hues. They produce white sand, which is used at London, Bristol, and Worcester, in the composition of the finer sorts of glass and porcelain.'* - History of the Isle of Wight, Worsley, 1781.

12 Seagrove Bay.
A lovely study of a beach scene 100 years ago, taken by Hogg, no doubt with a view to selling it as a postcard, but also taken by a man who clearly had an eye for a good, strong photograph. Despite the houses in the photograph having been lost to the blue slipper clay, Seagrove Bay with Horestone Point in the background still looks very similar today, and has kept its charm despite the recent coastal defence works that have taken place.

13 Pier Road, Seaview.
These ladies are sitting on a wall opposite the Halland Hotel, just out of view on the left. Today, both have gone, only the house in the distance remaining, and where the Halland once stood there are now apartments. The name of the road remains, unchanged in a nod to the past. In August 1969, this wall was photographed again, but more famously this time, with Bob Dylan sitting precisely where the ladies are sitting, prior to his appearance at the Wootton Festival.

14 The Slipway, Seaview.
In 1910, the photographer obviously went to some effort to get the picture he wanted, having clambered out onto the rocks, risking his valuable equipment. Some houses have changed but the location remains instantly recognisable.

15 Seagrove Bay, Seaview.
This is the slipway at Seagrove Bay looking towards Seaview, with Horestone Point behind the camera. To the locals' relief, no doubt, Seagrove is not the easiest of places to find or get to, having no direct road access and strictly no parking. Consequently Seagrove still has the best of both worlds. It has an air of exclusivity but is still pleasantly busy; mainly with locals, but also with a few determined outsiders who make their way on foot.

16 Seaview Pier.
Opened in 1881, the pier made between £500 and £900 a year from day trips and ferry services. The railway companies soon took this trade away and, as the years went by, income dwindled, until in 1947 the pier was sold, raising only £775. In 1948, red tape over restoration led the new owner to announce its demolition. After uproar, the pier was listed in 1950 but, ironically, only four weeks later, nature achieved what the owner had intended and in just 48 hours Christmas storms washed the pier away for ever.

17 The Toll Road, Seaview.
The track and wall in front of the houses was put there in 1790 to breach the mouth of Barnsley Harbour, which, until silting up, had stretched inland at that point. The road from Puckpool to Seaview was not laid on top of it until early in the 20th century, just after this photograph was taken. Until recent times it remained a toll road, with a manned tollbooth at the Puckpool end. Prior to its opening, the trip from Ryde could only be made using an inconvenient inland route via Nettlestone.

18 PS *Duchess of Kent* leaving Ryde Pier.
The *Duchess of Kent* was licensed to carry 870 passengers and from the look of her in this photograph she isn't far off that figure. Built for Red Funnel in 1890, specifically to operate on the Portsmouth to Ryde passenger service, she was sold in 1933 to work out of Blackpool and was scrapped in 1937. Piers and their attractions were immensely popular in their heyday as the number of people here clearly demonstrates, but tastes changed, and slowly, Britain's piers began their decline.

19 Crowds on Ryde Pier.
At the time this photograph was taken, Ryde actually had two piers. The smaller Victoria Pier nearby, built in 1863, had fallen into disuse and was bought by Ryde Borough Council in 1914. Due to the popularity of the railway pier and its attractions, Victoria Pier became an unused liability and was demolished in 1916.

20 Day Trippers, Ryde Pier.
Judging from the number of flags that are flying, this photograph was possibly taken during one of the annual Fleet Reviews; perhaps the 1911 Coronation Review. Whether the people in this superb photograph are day-trippers returning from Portsmouth or simply out on the pier to see the Review, is not known. The two couples laughing and the girl staring intently into the camera offered a perfect moment in time to be captured from the long hot summer before the imminent war.

21 PS *Lorna Doone*.
On the seas for 60 years, the *Lorna Doone* was built in 1891 and in 1898 became the property of the Southampton, IOW and South of England Royal Mail Steam Packet Co., whose more familiar name was, and is, Red Funnel. For many years she generated large profits, operating packed trips from Southampton to Bournemouth and Swanage via the Isle of Wight. She did military service in the two wars, as a minesweeper both times, and was finally scrapped in 1948.

22 *PS Prince of Wales*.
Another Red Funnel ship, she was built in 1891. In 1896 she collided with Clarence Pier and in 1903 collided with a submarine in Portsmouth Harbour. Another collision followed in 1927 when she hit a yacht and in 1934 she collided with PS *Princess Helena*. Finally, in her last collision in 1935, she hit and sank the yacht *Robin*, drowning her skipper. She was scrapped in 1938. Hopefully this was one of her luckier trips.

23 Garden Archway, Unknown Location.
An unknown location but probably in the Ryde area. Taken by W.R.Hogg it exhibits perfect composition and flawless exposure and was included in a series of photographs of high status residences of that area. If anyone should recognise the location, please let us know via the publisher.

24 Fernhill House, Wootton.
Set in the rolling fields above Lakeside, it met an unfortunate end one hot summer's day in June 1938 when a stray spark from a workman's bonfire set fire to some roofing material. In just one hour, the house, and most of its contents, were totally destroyed *'It is in a style not calculated to convey a favourable idea of the erector's taste. It is <u>meant</u> to be Gothic but the general aspect is church-like'* - Barbers Picturesque Guide, 1845.

25 and 26 House Interior, Unknown Location.
When this room was photographed, in around 1905, most of the furniture was already 150 years old and the contemporary content is virtually nil. The matching chairs, bookcase, and writing desk, for example, probably date from the reign of George II (1727-60). The room, in an early Victorian house, *circa* 1840, suggests wealth and stature and is hung with tasteful etchings, watercolours and prints. To fill a room with these items today would cost £30-£50,000.

27 Theatre Royal, Ryde.
With seating for 1,000, a lavish interior and high-class productions featuring household names, this was one of the top theatres in the South of England, and had flourished since the late 18th century. The 1900s saw theatres begin to lose their audiences to cinemas and in the 1940s the Theatre Royal itself became a cinema in order to survive. Sadly it burnt down in the 1960s to be replaced by the Nat West Bank. The Pearl White film advertised on the billboard was released in 1918.

28 The Royal Victoria Yacht Club, Ryde.
The RVYC moved to Fishbourne in 1966 and as more than one generation of young Islanders will know, the building became The Prince Consort, a watering hole with meals and music. Later generations will know it as 'Patsy's' or T.J's gym. *'The Royal Victoria Yacht Club is perhaps the best known yacht club in the world after the Royal Yacht Squadron at Cowes. Their Ryde regatta is one of the events of the year.'* - 1912 Tourist Guide.

29 St Thomas Square and Union Street, Ryde.
On the right, at the top of Union Street is Ryde Post Office and on the roof overhead telephone lines converge on a gantry before making their way down into Ryde's new telephone exchange. It was opened by the National Telephone Company in 1897, with 70 customers who had agreed to pay between £8 and £10 annual line rental. The calls, made via an operator, cost a penny each. Five years later, the number of subscribers had more than doubled.

30 River Medina, St Cross, Newport.
This photograph, looking eastwards from Towngate Bridge at the bottom of Hunny Hill, shows Mew Langton's brewery in the distance, sited opposite the Medina Railway pub. The brewery was demolished after a fire in December 1980 and the site is now St. Cross Court. To the right of the photograph, the bushes, trees and dilapidated buildings are in what is now the car park for Halfords and Brantano. In the river are the sluice gates for St Cross Mill which can still be seen today.

31 Little London, Newport.
This 1924 view is looking towards Cowes. On the western bank is the derrick hoist belonging to Shepard Bros used to unload goods from ships into the Derrick Store, now The Bargeman's Rest. Further down the Quay is the Model Stores, also belonging to Shepard Bros., now converted into flats. On the eastern side, Leigh Thomas' grain store is under construction. Changing hands in 1934, it was later renamed the Jubilee Stores to mark the silver jubilee of George V, by its new owner Crouchers, the carriers.

32 The Harbour, Newport.
Seen here around 1900. The first boat on the left is the locally based *Gazelle* and on the opposite bank is the steam ship *Spray*, owned by Shepard Bros. '*A TABLE OF ASSESSMENTS For The Carriage of Goods to Newport, - Anchovies, per barrel 6d., Bottles (empty) per doz., 2d.,Brushes, small per doz., 1½d., Gunpowder per barrel, 1s 0d., Nuts per bag, 8d., Soap per firkin, 6d., Tallow, English, per hogshead, 4s 6d.*' - Extract from an 1872 Act of Parliament, listing tariffs on goods landed at Newport.

33 River Medina, Dodnor.
In this photograph from the early 1900s, the boy is standing on the east bank of the Medina in today's Seaclose Park where this inlet can still be identified. On the horizon is the Cowes to Newport railway line and below it what is now the picnic area at Riverway. The line closed in 1966 and in later years the redundant trackbed became the cycleway to Cowes. The boy appears to be using a quarter-plate camera, similar to those that would have been used to take some of the photographs in this book.

34 Cargo Ship, River Medina.
Unfortunately, no amount of enhancement could reveal the name of this ship. It is moored just off the Medina Jetty, presumably having business there. The Jetty appears to be a different one to that shown in plate 80.

35 The Black Horse Inn, George Street, Ryde.
Sailor suits were fashionable for many children. Did they and their mother know the photographer or did they simply happen to be there when he took the photograph? A baker's bread cart alongside bears the name, 'Hazard - Baker, Ryde'. The Black Horse Inn on the corner is actually 9, Castle Street. It opened in 1828 and ended its days as a Mew Langton's pub; finally closing its doors in 1972.

36 Pier Street, Ryde.
The building on the left, not easy to place with modern eyes, is the Royal Pier Hotel which was demolished in 1932 (*see Plate 3*). On the right, still very much in existence is the King Lud pub. Brickwoods, the Portsmouth brewery, owned many Island pubs until the 1960s and several of them, including the King Lud, were given the mock Tudor treatment. Accordingly, it dates not from the early 1600s but more modestly, from the early 1900s.

37 The Hand in Hand, Nelson Place, Ryde.
The children standing below the lantern are outside 9, Nelson Place, otherwise known as the Hand in Hand public house. It opened in 1869 and despite a reputation of being haunted, it managed to stay in business for nearly 60 years until it closed in 1928. In the far distance, is a glimpse of Victoria Pier, which for a while, co-existed with the later railway pier.

38 The New Inn, Brighstone
The sign above the pub door says, 'Job Hawker. Licensed to retail Beer, Spirits and Tobacco - Luncheons and Teas - Motors For Hire - Good Accommodation For Cyclists.' Brighstone's village inn was originally The Five Bells until it moved to a new building when it was inevitably renamed The New Inn and then in 1973 became The Three Bishops.

39 The Fleming Arms, Binstead.
In 1606, Sir Thomas Fleming was one of the judges who condemned Guy Fawkes and his fellow plotters to death. He was also happened to be a Newport man who lived in the High Street on the corner of St Thomas Square. He was the first of a long line of Flemings who owned estates and land on the Island over the next 350 years. He could never have dreamt that one day a family member would have a Binstead pub named after him.

40 Lower High Street, Ryde.
This part of the High Street has not changed much in a hundred years. On the left is the Prince of Wales pub (*see Plate 41*) whose upper bay windows can apparently still be seen today. They are, in fact, only replicas as the building was, in recent years, extensively rebuilt. It is now the frontage of Hargreaves Sports Wear.

41 The Prince of Wales, High Street, Ryde.
On this site stood one of Ryde's oldest buildings. Known as Dagwell's Bargain after Edward Dagwell, who lived there in the 17th century, it occupied this plot until the Prince of Wales pub was built here in 1846. The poster on the right, of an emaciated horse declares, 'England's Disgrace' and is advertising a meeting of the Dumb Friends League while the other, ironically, is for Pearce's 'Royal Blue Coaches' horse-drawn excursion trips.

42 The Vine, Ryde.

Located at 16 Castle Street, it opened as the Globe in 1859 and became The Vine when a new owner, Thomas Saunders, brought the name with him from his old pub. He was also a builder of some note who went on to build the Victoria Arcade in Union Street. The Vine eventually suffered the fate of many other former Mew Langton's pubs at that time and was closed in a corporate purge in 1971. The building is currently a guesthouse.

43 The Strand Hotel, Ryde.

The pub was originally built and known as the Strand Hotel. A model of a flat iron stood on the roof for many years reflecting the fact that the pub was built on a 'flat iron' shaped site. Perhaps inevitably, the nickname took over and 'The Flat Iron' became its new name in 1974. It closed as a pub in the early 1980s and is now a Chinese take away.

44 The Hare and Hounds, Arreton.

There is no clue as to why this photograph was taken. Across the road is 'Michal Morey's hump'. He killed a boy in 1735 and was hanged at Winchester. His body was returned to the Island and hung in a gibbet here for the birds to pick clean. Two hundred years later, a skull was found in the hump and is still displayed in the pub, labelled as being that of Morey. Archaeologists have more realistically pronounced it to be that of a pre-historic girl in her late teens.

45 The White Lion, Niton.

'Niton or, as it is sometimes called, Crab Niton, occupies a very secluded situation. It is a village of considerable antiquity, consisting in the main of two small streets of stone houses, some with thatched roofs. There is a small inn in the village and a number of cottages furnished for lodgings. It has, moreover, several excellent houses and a considerable population.' - Nelson's Guide Book, 1859.

46 Advertisement Hoarding, St John's Road Bridge, Ryde .

This lovely photograph is one of a series of the same hoarding taken over a period of months. They were commissioned by the advertising agent to be shown to clients as proof of display. In a testament to the power of advertising, most of the products advertised are still in production 100 years on. On the extreme right are the arches of St John's Road Bridge and in the distance is Oakfield. Behind the hoarding a livestock auction is in progress in Ryde Market Repository.

47 Evans & Dyke, Ryde.

On close examination, the contents of Evans and Dyke's shop window a hundred years ago don't appear that different to the contents of a modern jeweller's shop window. Located then at 24 Cross Street, Evans and Dyke traded in Ryde for many years and were still listed as 'Evans, E.J., watchmaker', in a street directory of 1924. By 1931, the shop had been re-numbered as No. 28. Today, virtually unrecognisable, the site is now home to The Coffee Bar.

48 The Dore Sisters, Warwick Street, Ryde.

In the 1881 census the Dore family is shown living at 3 Warwick Street with three boys and six daughters. This photograph, some 25 years on, shows how some of the sisters had prospered with their house furnishing and employment agency business which now occupied 2, 3, 4, 5, 6 and 7 Warwick Street. As late as 1924 a street directory lists various Dores in Ryde in trades as diverse as Servant Registry, Ironmonger and, bizarrely, Firewood Dealer.

49 Temperance Hotel, Ryde.

This is 5 Union Street, now Dos Amigos restaurant, and was just one of Ryde's many temperance hotels. A hundred years ago, drinking was a large social problem affecting all classes of society from the top to the bottom. The temperance movement flourished and their millions of members took the pledge to shun alcohol. Hotels and restaurants like this one quickly sprang up to fill the need for meals and accommodation in alcohol free surroundings.

50 Washhouse, Unknown Location.

A lovely photograph of an obviously busy laundry, perhaps in a large residence. The plate has unfortunately suffered permanent water damage. It is one of a batch that had apparently been kept in an open wooden box in a wet outhouse. They were removed in time to save some but many of the other images had been damaged beyond repair. The vignetting, or darkening of the corners, is caused by the use of a lens designed for use on a smaller format camera.

51 Railway Agents, George Street, Ryde.

Railway travel was enjoying a boom, so much so that on the corners of George Street, the railway companies LBSCR and LSWR found it worth their while to open agencies. In 1897 the Island lines alone carried 1½ million passengers. *'Two days race traffic at Ashey will bring 3,000, while 600 will turn out freely for a football match between rival towns. 7,000 will take up an excursion booking between Newport and Cowes in the summer and 2,000 will book at Newport in a single day on a popular festival.'* - The Railway Magazine, March 1899.

52 Pickfords Office, Esplanade, Ryde.
This was situated to the right of the entrance to Ryde Esplanade station and W.H.Smith's, the stationers. The two employees posing at the door, who have obviously been called out for the occasion and the impressive display of travel posters makes a perfect photograph. The I.W. Central Railway poster is advertising weekly tickets at 5/- (7/6d, 1st class) for travel on the Central Line only, or 14/6d, (20/-, 1st class) for a joint ticket allowing travel on all three of the Island's lines.

53 Heath's Store, The Broadway, Totland.
A nicely posed photograph with human interest and a glimpse into a shop window full of cakes, chocolate and sweet jars nearly one hundred years ago. This was No.1 The Broadway, Totland, on the western side of the road near today's roundabout. Although the shop front has now long gone and the shop has been converted into a house, evidence of where the awning brackets and shop sign were fixed to the wall can still be seen.

54 Lower Union Street, Ryde.
Until the 1780s, Ryde was two separate entities. At the top of the town was a village on the site of today's High Street, while the bottom of the town was just a small fishing port. Linking the two were paths down through a 12 acre wooded field called Node Close. In 1780 one of these paths was staked out into plots and given the name Union Street. In 1797, Mr Yelf opened a wine shop here, and in 1810, a hotel. The rest of Union Street rapidly followed.

55 St John's Road Bridge, Ryde.
The ladies emerging from Monkton Street (right) are passing the Terminus Hotel, so named because until 1880 St Johns Road station was the terminus of the lines from Cowes and Ventnor, the line to Ryde Pier not yet being built. The pub across the road in Monkton Street has traded under the names The Railway Commercial, The Monkton House Inn, The Railway Inn, The Hole in the Wall, and The Cask and Cucumber. For the moment, however, it is just The Railway.

56 Upper High Street, Ryde.
A clear demonstration of the power of the camera 100 years ago. Of the 25 or so people in this photograph, around 20 of them have actually stopped what they are doing to stare intently at the camera and photographer. The surrounding buildings are unchanged for the most part and a hundred years later the Post Office still survives in the same premises but now trading as Mellish's.

57 The High Street, Carisbrooke.
This is not quite the timeless picture it first seems. The Red Lion has gone, to be transformed into housing and the Castle is now a supermarket. On the right, the block of terraced cottages has long since been demolished and the site now forms the entrance to the village car park. The Eight Bells coaching yard can be seen with its arched entrance, the remnants of which are still there today. Propped against the walls of both the Eight Bells and the Castle are the ladders used for reaching the top deck of horse-drawn coaches.

58 Castle Street Ford, Carisbrooke.
At one time, the flow of the River Medina provided the motive power for eight corn mills, set between Clatterford and St Cross at Hunny Hill. In this photograph, the river has just passed through Kent Mill, out of shot, to the left of the picture and is on its way to Priory Mill. Both of these buildings are still in existence.

59 The Church and Bell Inn, Godshill.
There are many chocolate box photographs of Godshill church in existence and another one seems superfluous but we have had to make an exception here because on close inspection, this is a much rarer picture than is first apparent. The cottage on the right was, at the time, The Bell Inn. The landlady of the house is standing in the porch, under the pub sign, a picture of a bell. Outside, a man poses for the photographer with his rip hook.

60 High Street and Square, Brading.
One of the ill-fated IOW Motor Express Syndicate buses limps up the hill into the square. 'Brading's one and only street straggles up a steep hill to the church. The doorways are mostly flush with the pavement and afford every convenience for friendly gossip. If the coaches would only keep away, Brading would go to sleep very comfortably' - Ward Lock Guide Book 1912.

61 IWCR Railway Station, Shide.
The station was reported as 'all but completed', in November 1874 when the contractor's engine ran over the newly completed line from Shide to Sandown 'in pouring rain and a chill wind'. It opened to the public two months later. The Central remained solvent, generating modest profits all its life. It was sold in 1923 to the Southern Railway, according to its Chairman, 'in a higher state of efficiency and with greater promise than at any time in its history', the Directors receiving £5,000 compensation each for loss of office.

62 Binstead Hill.
It is fair to say that Binstead has changed a great deal since this was taken. The church remains but has been converted into residential accommodation; and the Forge, to the left of the church is still there for those who look hard enough. The hill, though, has changed almost beyond recognition and now has an unbroken line of bungalows and houses on the left and, as the residents will no doubt testify, an unbroken line of traffic on the road.

63 Denmark Road School, Cowes.
This 1907 photograph, showing Denmark Road School being built, will stir the memories of many Cowes inhabitants. The minutes of Cowes Local Board show that Denmark Road was adopted as a highway in 1906 and that the school was built in 1907. It survived into the 1990s when it was demolished to become a temporary car park. In 2004, an imposing block of apartments was built on the site.

64 and 65 Views from St Thomas Church, Newport.
These are just two of a series of photographs in our collection of a 360° panorama of Newport in October 1927. In plate 64, the large building, top centre, is Mew Langton's brewery and to its right an arch leads into the railway station. Left of that is the old brewery in Crocker Street, complete with oast houses. In plate 65, at top, centre left, is a pole routing lines into the telephone exchange in the High Street Post Office. To the left of the pole is the Grand cinema in Lugley Street, now single storey. Further left is the Rink cinema, originally built for roller skating.

66 The Toll Bridge, Yarmouth.
To cross the River Yar had always meant a ferryboat trip with all its inconveniences but in 1863 the Yar Bridge Company opened its new toll bridge. To cross at a penny per person was a bargain, while mules cost a penny and donkeys or horses were two pence. The bridge was an immediate success and the shareholders enjoyed 70 prosperous years until the Council purchased the bridge in 1934 and freed it from tolls. The building on the right is the toll collector's house.

67 The Square, Yarmouth.
It is 27 minutes past 3 on a quiet summer's afternoon. Out of shot on the left is the Jubilee Oak of 1897 and the visible tree is the Coronation Oak of 1902. Both trees were hopelessly ill placed for the coming age of the motor car and had predictably short lives. The Bugle pub and Harwoods were in existence even in the 1920s when this photograph was taken. Just to the left of the church clock, a man sits on the ridge of the church roof carrying out repairs.

68 The Royal Spithead Hotel, Bembridge.
The hotel, built by the owners of the Brading to Bembridge railway, opened in 1882. By 1953 when the line closed, the hotel had seen better times and eventually closed. It re-opened as Greyland's College for a short while but was bought by developers and demolished in 1989. A block of flats now graces the site. *'If you care for a place where the evening occupations are as nearly as possible nil ... and where the only excitement is the arrival of a railway train, then Bembridge is not likely to disappoint.'* - Ward Lock Guide Book 1912.

69 The High Street, Sandown.
This is the turn of the last century at Sandown before tourism had taken over and changed the face of the High Street. Unlike today, the shops were selling practical household necessities, displays overflowing onto the pavement outside. The people in the foreground are staring at the photographer, again showing what an event the simple taking of a photograph could be.

70 The High Street, Newport.
Newport decked out for the Queen's visit to celebrate her diamond jubilee of 1897. What it lacks technically is more than made up by its content. On the right is the Antelope Inn, rarely, if ever, photographed. It closed in 1908 and was eventually incorporated behind Dabell's shop front, when they occupied the site. The interior remained intact but unsung within Dabell's but with the coming of BHS has disappeared forever.

71 The Town Hall, Newport.
Another rare glimpse of some Newport shops prior to the Queen's visit. The people outside the town hall are inspecting a large display of electric lights being installed. Newport did not have electricity at that time so this display was probably one of several temporary illuminations known to have been installed across the Island especially for the Jubilee celebration

72 St Thomas Square, Newport.
Frustratingly for such an interesting photograph, we know nothing about what is taking place here. Accompanying negatives of the same event show the children, a few moments before, lined up on the pavement complete with labels around their necks, awaiting the arrival of the cars which they are now sitting in. The event, in the mid-1920s, is of sufficient interest to bring the adults in the Square to a halt.

73 Railway Viaduct, Newport

This was taken from the top of St Thomas church, looking down Pyle Street in 1898. The large building at the bottom of Pyle Street is Ford Mill, demolished in 1962. The site is now part of the roundabout. A double-headed train is crossing the viaduct into Newport, having come from Sandown. Behind, are Robin Hood Street and Barton village and construction has started on Ash Road. The fields disappearing up into the distance have since become Pan Estate.

74 FY&N Railway Station, Carisbrooke.

'Passengers on the last train on Sunday evening had an unpleasant and rather alarming experience. All went well till Carisbrooke station, shortly after 8 o'clock, when instead of keeping to the main track, the train went off on to the siding, crashing into five chalk-laden trucks standing there. Mr Harley, the temporary station master stated that he was positive the points were all right when he left the signal-box to book passengers. He alleged that someone must have tampered with the points in his absence.' - IWCP 22nd September, 1894.

75 FY&N Railway Station, Calbourne.

This is a rare photograph of Calbourne station in its early days, taken in about 1898. At the rear of the platform is an unusual elevated siding. The station, located in Elm Lane, became derelict following line closure in 1953 and was eventually demolished in the 1970s. The site today is occupied by a bungalow, Badger's Bend.

76 IWCR Railway Station, Newport.

IWCP Report of Council meeting, 26th May, 1894 - *'The Members and A Railway Company. - Mr. Fox said when they travelled on the line in a first-class carriage, if they took a waterproof and umbrella they could travel with fair safety and comfort..... Dr. Dabbs said the line was a dustbin on wheels (laughter).'* Contemporary cartoon of a railway poster - *'Isle of Wight railways; 12 miles in 12 hours for 12 shillings.'* Contemporary legend - *'The dog which fell out of the train window at Newport was waiting for the train on its arrival at Havenstreet.'*

77 Railway Tunnel, St Lawrence.

The tunnel that runs from Dean Farm at Whitwell to St Lawrence, was part of the Newport, Godshill and St Lawrence Railway and was blasted from the rock in 1896 using 500 lb. of gelignite. The contractor was fined £35 at Newport for not having proper storage facilities for it. The tunnel mouth, now bricked up, can still be seen today in the undergrowth just off public footpath V81 which leads to St Rhadegunds Path, a few metres north of its junction with Seven Sisters Road.

78 IWR Railway Station, Ventnor.

The station opened in 1866 on the site of a stone quarry. Some stone removal and cutting was still taking place in the 1920s. After early financial problems the line from Ryde became profitable, especially in the late 1800s, when it paid *'dividends as high as any paid by a railway company in Britain'*. It prospered for some 60 years until it was compulsorily taken over by the Southern Railway in 1923, who even then had to pay a healthy sum to the shareholders in compensation, reflecting its profitability.

79 Railway Crossing, Alvington.

This lovely photograph shows the occupation crossing at Alvington Manor Farm, Newport. The location can be found today on public footpath number N151. Amazingly, the gate shown in the photograph is still there, lying in the grass, albeit in a buckled state, beyond repair. On the opposite side of the track, nearer the camera, the remains of the wooden stile posts can still be clearly identified in the undergrowth today, after a hundred years.

80 Medina Railway Jetty, Cowes.

The profits of the IWC Railway were swelled by the revenue from goods traffic, most of which passed through Medina Jetty. It was constructed in 1878 by a joint committee of the Cowes & Newport and Ryde & Newport railways to carry a short goods siding out onto the river and went through several reincarnations during its life. We believe this one to be in the late 1890s. The wooden jetty lasted in one form or another until the replacement Medina Wharf was built in 1932. Note the railway wagons halfway along.

81 IWCR Railway Station, Cowes.

Photographs of Cowes railway station are not difficult to find but this one is an oddity perhaps, in that it shows the station under a layer of snow. It was taken from Granville Road Bridge in about 1900.

82 Union Street, Ryde.

This is almost certainly December 1908, when much of the Island was blanketed with heavy snow. The photograph is of the same snowfall shown in plate 84, Gilling's Shop at Freshwater.

83 Clifford's Gate, Spencer Road, Ryde.
This was originally taken by W.R. Hogg to be sold as a Christmas greetings postcard. The depth of snow in the photograph suggests it was taken during the severe winter of 1908. Clifford's Gate is a well known Ryde landmark, still in existence, which used to mark the entrance to Westfield, the home of the Clifford family.

84 Gilling's, Station Road, Freshwater.
Taken on 25th April, 1908, this is Station Road now renamed School Green Road, the building is still there today, currently vacant. Gillings also ran shops on The Broadway, Totland and The Avenue. *'Local Success – Mr. T. Gilling, the well known baker and confectioner of Station Road and Totland, has just recently been awarded a gold medal at London, in open competition, for purity of household bread baked in hygienic ovens.'* - Freshwater, Totland and Yarmouth Advertiser, 1st August, 1903.

85 The York Hotel, George Street, Ryde.
This was probably taken after the snowstorms that struck the Island in 1908. The building in the photograph was never intended to be a hotel but had been built as a private residence. In 1935 the current art deco building replaced it. As The Royal York, it was a popular venue in the 1960s, fondly remembered for appearances from acts as diverse as the Bonzo Dog Band and Gene Vincent.

86 The Hunt in St James Square, Newport.
In the mid-1920s when this photograph was taken, the Hunt formed a syndicate to fund the building of kennels at Gatcombe where they are still to be found. In 1925 the Island's fox population was threatened by an outbreak of mange. To safeguard hunting, it was decided to use badgers to drive the foxes from their contaminated earths. Badgers had been previously introduced to the Island in the 1840s but were extinct by 1909 and so the Hunt successfully re-introduced badgers to the Island by releasing some at Lynn Common.

87 The Hunt on The Downs.
Surprisingly, the Island had no foxes until 1843, when they were deliberately introduced specifically for the purpose of being hunted. The son of the Master of Harriers, tired of hunting hares, learned of eight foxes for sale at Portsmouth. He purchased them all and brought them over to the Island secretly, knowing that his father would not approve. He released them in woodland at Newchurch to provide a more exciting quarry for the hunt and their descendants have been here ever since.

88 The Hunt at Calbourne.
Lynch Lane, seen in about 1900. There were very few cars on the road and life was so much easier for the Isle of Wight Hunt. *'Walkelin Bishop of Winchester holds Calbourne in Lordship. Land for 25 ploughs. In Lordship 6 ploughs; 27 villagers and 15 smallholders with 14 ploughs.11 slaves; 2 mills at 6s 3d; meadow, 8 acres; woodland at 20 pigs. The value of the whole manor before 1066 and later was £16.'* - Domesday Book, 1085.

89 The Racecourse, Ashey
The Island has had several racecourses in its time; including Monkham, Appleford and this one, Ashey, which opened in 1882. Always popular, it survived until 1930 when the timber grandstand burnt down. The races were so well attended, with up to 3,000 visitors, that the IW Railway ran special trains to the event. Ashey station is just visible, with carriages parked in the racecourse siding. In 1941 the land was ploughed up for the war effort, and all trace of the racecourse disappeared.

90 Stuck in the Mud.
A splendid photograph, capturing not just a moment in time but close up details of the people's clothes and the car being pushed. From close examination of other negatives accompanying this one, we think the location is the racecourse at Ashey.

91 IWCR Rolling Stock, Newport.
This rolling stock is in sidings just outside Newport station on the line to Cowes. The carriages were the company's spare coaching stock at the time and were originally built for the London & Birmingham Railway in 1842. Most of these vehicles were withdrawn between 1904 and 1911. The photographer's vantage point is now the pavement outside Premier Ford on the Riverway industrial estate. The rooftop in the distance on the right is that of the Ship and Launch Inn. Across the river the inlet can just be made out where the children in plate 33 were photographed.

92 Bus Garage Fire, Somerton, Cowes.
The Vectis Bus Co. was just six years old when its garage at Cowes was destroyed by a fire that broke out in the small hours of 2nd October, 1927. With perfect ingredients and a strong wind to fan it, the night shift staff were powerless to stop the fire, which was rumoured to have been started by a carelessly thrown match. Over 30 buses were garaged there that night and 13 of them were lost. The building itself lives on today as the depot of 'Steve Porter Transport'.

93 Roman Villa, Newport.
In 1926, foundations for a house were being dug in Cypress Road. The Council Inspector was examining the trench and saw what he thought might be Roman tiles. He called in the Curator of Carisbrooke Castle who confirmed his suspicions and the next day mosaic floors were found. The County Press started a fund to finance excavations and an anonymous benefactor purchased the site, safeguarding its future. The men here have cleaned the site prior to the new building being erected

94 The Keep, Carisbrooke Castle.
Although times may change, tourists are tourists. The keep of Carisbrooke Castle has attracted countless thousands of them in the past, and always will. Children will probably always count the steps to the top and then drop things down the well in the keep when no one is looking.

95 Abbey Ruins, Quarr.
After it was closed by Henry VIII and the 10 resident priests had left, the Abbey was demolished and in an irony not lost on the King the stone was used to build his castles at East and West Cowes, now both gone. Yarmouth Castle contains reclaimed stone, some with mediaeval carvings which, *'ultimately derive from a monastic building'*. It is possible that these are corbels from Quarr. They can still be seen through a glass plate set in one of the upstairs floors of Yarmouth castle.

96 IW Museum, Quay Street, Newport.
The Isle of Wight Museum was, for years, located next door to Calvert's Hotel in Quay Street. There is an impressive amount of exhibits on display here begging the question of their current whereabouts. In 1912, Ward Lock's Guide to the Island informed readers that, *'The Museum at 30, Quay Street is open from 11 to 4 daily, admission is 3d.'*

97 Beach Scene, Unknown Location.
An unknown location in the mid-1920s, but probably Shanklin beach photographed from the pier. Something in the sea is plainly attracting the attention of the people at the top left. As usual for those times, most people on the beach look overdressed to our eyes. The length and direction of the shadows suggest a midsummer evening. In the midst of the crowd, a man sits playing a harmonium.

98 The Cascade, Ventnor.
The archways are hiding nature's original cliff edge, from where a spring still originates and nowadays hidden in a culvert, runs to the sea. Until the late 19th century the flowing spring drove a water mill on the site which had been there in one form or another since at least the 13th century. A street guide for 1867 lists the last ever miller as a Mr Davis. Only the arches remain today, a shadow of their former glory. The pretty gardens are long gone, buried under cement.

99 The Carnival, Ventnor.
'Look at the plan of Ventnor: the few streets which run up-hill from the sea are as higgledy-piggledy as well can be.... The stranger who reaches Ventnor by rail will naturally first ask how he is to get to the sea. The simplest way is to go steadily down – where you can go steadily – till you come to it.' - Ward Lock Guide Book 1912.

100 Old Soldier and Dog
A very evocative 1920s photograph of an old man with possibly the only things he has of any value in his life, his dog and his medals. He is unknown, unfortunately, but because he has put his medals on for the photographer we are able tell a little about him and his life. From left to right, the campaign medals are from Afghanistan 1878-80, Egypt 1882-89, and the Khedives Bronze Star of 1882-91.

101 St Boniface Church, Bonchurch.
A beautiful W.R. Hogg photograph. The glass negative is of very high contrast, producing a print that is suitably stark and almost gothic. *'The parish church is of rude and simple character and of ancient date. Shaded by venerable elms, it is of Norman design and is beautifully situated in the midst of rocks and foliage.'* - Nelson's Handbook for Tourists, 1859.

102 The Regatta, Seaview.
The annual Regatta, taking place in the shadow of Seaview Pier. *'Seaview Pier has some claim to be considered unique in that it is undeniably handsome. The pier-head is sufficiently roomy for three vessels to lie alongside at the same time. Four standards support the pier by means of wire ropes, instead of the usual chains, and several ingenious devices lessen the oscillation usually attendant upon such structures. Steamers call frequently from Southampton, Bournemouth etc.'* - Ward Lock Guide Book 1912

Abbreviations

FY&N   Freshwater, Yarmouth and Newport Railway
IWR   Isle of Wight Railway
IWCR   Isle of Wight Central Railway
IWCP   Isle of Wight County Press
LBSCR   London, Brighton & South Coast Railway
LSWR   London & South Western Railway
PS   Paddle Steamer

Bibliography

Footlights and Silver Screen, P. Norris, Island Books, 1998.

Isle of Wight Photographers, R.V. Turley, University of Southampton, 2001.

Isle of Wight Central Railway, R.J. Maycock and R. Silsbury, The Oakwood Press, 2001.

Newport Remembered, Bill Shepard, IW Natural History and Archaeological Society, 1984.

Picturesque Illustrations of the Isle of Wight, Barber, Simpkin and Marshall, 1845.

Piers of the Isle of Wight, M. Lane, Isle of Wight Council, 1996.

Quarr Abbey and Its Lands, S.F. Hockey, Leicester University Press, 1970.

Romans on the Wight, Cultural Services, IW County Council, 1992.

Ryde Pubs, K. Mitchell, Kena Publishing, 1999.

The History of the Isle of Wight, Sir Richard Worsley, 1781.

The Island From Within, R. Sawyer, Robook Publications, 1990.

The Manor Houses of the Isle of Wight, C.W.R. Winter, Forget-Me-Not Books, 1991.

The Mills of The Isle of Wight, J. Kenneth Major, Charles Skilton Ltd, 1970.

The Natural History of the Isle of Wight, Oliver Frazer, Dovecote Press, 1990.

The Isle of Wight County Press, Various.

The Isle of Wight, Illustrated Guide Book, Ward Lock & Co., 1912.

The Isle of Wight, Nelson's Handbook For Tourists, 1859.

The Isle of Wight Rifles, D.J. Quigley, Quigley, 1976.

Wight: Biography of an Island, P. Hyland, Gollancz, 1985.

Wight Report Railway Magazine, Isle of Wight Railway Co. Ltd, Various.

Wight Wires, M. Bird, Olympia Publishing, 1996.

Yarmouth Castle, Guide Leaflet, HMSO, 1959.

Yarmouth, Isle of Wight, A.G. Cole, Isle of Wight County Press, 1946.

Technical Notes

The half-plate negatives were scanned using an Agfa 1236u Scanner with an A4 transparency adapter and the quarter-plate negatives were scanned using an Epson 1640su scanner. The resulting image files were restored and prepared for publication using Adobe Photoshop 7.

Acknowledgements

Steve Colebrook, Richard Brimson, John Frampton, Stephen Gratton, John Groves, Ian Kennedy, Jane Kennedy, Rob Martin, Richard Maycock, Wayne Pritchett, Gerald Wildish.

Graphic Design and Layout by the authors.

Contact

High-quality prints on photographic paper, from images in this book, are available in various sizes. Please e-mail *isleofwightrevisited@yahoo.co.uk* to request further details. If you have any candidates for inclusion in any further publication, please contact the same e-mail address.